The Birds of Trinidad and Tobago

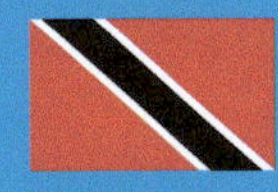 Nikeisha Jones

____

Publishing Support by Amazel Enterprise
www.amazelenterprise.com
publishingsupport@amazelenterprise.com
Cover and Interior Design by: Arbëresh Dalipi
+1868 346 8616

I would like to dedicate this book to my parents
and sister who are my biggest supporters.

A special thank you to Eureka Natural History Tours
and Nerissa Boyce as well.

It's the first day of vacation in Tobago
And my dad works in tourism as a bird guide
I've learnt a thing or two from him
So let me teach you, just stay by my side.

From my bedroom window this morning
On my window sill
What did I see?
A copper rumped hummingbird
Fluttering around my feeder
Like flowers and nectar are to the honeybee

I wanted to take a photo of it
But my weary eyes could barely see
For they are the fastest of all the
birds and many animals
Even faster than you and me

I went to the patio to have breakfast and whilst there
What did I see?
A bird with a breast as yellow as the sun
It was a magnificent Keskidee

The bird was rummaging through Rufus' bowl
And seemed to enjoy the dog chow
Why would such a distinguished looking bird eat dog food and insects
All day I wondered – How?

After breakfast Dad and I went to the park
And whilst there, what did we see?
About a dozen or so ruddy ground doves
All hopping around so peacefully

They were a dull brown colour
Less colourful than their counterparts previously
But they had the cutest little faces with a gentle disposition
And they cooed so harmoniously.

To grandma's house we went for lunch
And whilst there in the backyard, what did we see?
The rufus vented chachalaca also known as the Cocrico
A delightfully noisy bird indeed.

It is one of the national birds of Trinidad and Tobago
And a common bird in South America too
It looks like a brown chicken with a very long tail
But unlike the ruddy ground dove, it doesn't know how to coo.

My dad surprised me with tickets to Trinidad

And we had to fly the following day

He had to do a tour at the Caroni Bird Sanctuary

So it was only for a short stay.

The next day, the flight took only twenty minutes
And on arrival I was as happy as can be
Not only to be on the big sister isle
But I get to continue on this path of discovery

On a drive to the Caroni Bird Sanctuary
Such a beautiful day, what did I see?
An ornate hawk eagle
How majestic and splendorous was he

He dipped and soared elegantly
As he scoured diligently for prey
But my heart was broken when dad told me he feeds on smaller birds
And it almost ruined my day.

We arrived at the Caroni Bird Sanctuary
And whilst there, what did we see?
Another beautiful bird, the Scarlet Ibis
The other national bird of T&T.

These birds are my favourite colour
And my favourite colour is red
At dusk from the boat, they returned to nest
One by one, flying over my head.

I even saw Caribbean flamingos
Up until then I had only seen them in books
All in pink splendour, their legs like pink stilts
An extraordinary bird; such a charming look!

To add to the line up in the Caroni Bird Sanctuary
Stood the lanky egret with finesse
With their extended sharp bill and their lily white colour
And their long necks, the shape of an 'S'.

We went back to the hotel that evening
I had a long day and I needed to rest

Tomorrow we would head back home to Tobago
Going back home is always the best.

The next morning I arose at the crack of dawn
And from the balcony, what did I see?
It was a little Mot Mot, through the trees
Staring right back at me.

A pretty little bird with a racket tipped tail

In a perfect blend of colour

But I had to get ready to catch my flight

So I told it goodbye and jumped in the shower.

In the car park of the nature resort
We waited for our taxi
But my wandering eyes looked for more birds
And to my surprise, what did I see?

This time it was the blue-grey tanager
Also known as the blue jean
The colour of blue just like the sky above
And a songbird of the tanager team.

My beautiful country Trinidad and Tobago
Is home to almost 480 species of birds
One day I would be as knowledgeable as my dad
And my book would have many more words.

Thanks for coming along for the adventure.
Hope you were able to learn about some of our birds.

Birds of Trinidad and Tobago
from the book

- Copper rumped hummingbird

- Great Keskidee

- Ruddy Ground Dove

- Ornate Hawk Eagle

- Rufus Vented Chachalaca (Cocrico)

- Scarlet Ibis

- Caribbean Flamingo

- Egret

- Mot Mot

- Blue-grey tanager